KIDS MAKE PIZZA
40 FUN & EASY RECIPES!

MARIAN BUCK-MURRAY

PRIMA PUBLISHING

Created and produced with Prima Publishing by Storey Communications, Inc.,
    Schoolhouse Road, Pownal, Vermont 05261.
Storey Communications, Inc. Editor: Amanda R. Haar
Cover design: Lindy Dunlavey, The Dunlavey Studio, Sacramento
Cover illustration: © 1994, Mike Lester
Text design and production: Carol Jessop, Black Trout Design
Text illustrations: Jeff Shelly

Library of Congress Cataloging-in-Publication Data
Buck-Murray, Marian
    Kids make pizza : 40 fun & easy recipes / Marian Buck-Murray.
            p.   cm.
        Includes index.
        ISBN 1-55958-649-4
        1. Pizza—Juvenile literature. [1. Pizza. 2. Cookery.] I. Title.
    TX770.P58B83 1995
    641.8'24—dc20   94-32640
95 96 97 98 99 RRD 10 9 8 7 6 5 4 3 2 1
Printed in the United States of America

How to Order:
Single copies may be ordered from Prima Publishing, P.O. Box 1260BK, Rocklin, CA 95677; telephone (916) 632-4400. Quantity discounts are also available. On your letterhead, include information concerning intended use of books and the number you wish to purchase.

DEDICATION

In loving memory of my fun-loving sister, Charlotte Elizabeth Buck.

ACKNOWLEDGMENTS

Special thanks to the kids who worked hard to test the recipes for this book: Connor Allen, Charlotte Burkly, Molly Gilman, Annika Murray, Tara Nyhuis, and Josh Sussman. And thanks also to Rosalie Twist Murray for timing her birth so perfectly.

TABLE OF CONTENTS
IMPORTANT ILLUSTRATED TECHNIQUES ARE LISTED IN BOLD

v

PIZZA POINTERS

What's more fun than eating pizza at your favorite pizzeria? Making pizza of course! *Kids Make Pizza* is stuffed with recipes for gooey, chewy, crunchy, munchy, hot and spicy pizza pies. You'll learn how to mix and knead, stretch and roll, squish and smash, and toast and bake to create the perfect pizza pie. So roll up your sleeves, and turn your kitchen into one primo pizzeria!

LET'S GET COOKING!

Before you begin any pizza project always remember to wash your hands, and tie back long hair if you have it. Since making pizza is a messy project, you'll probably want to wear an apron.

Here are a few more things to remember:

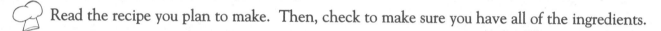 Read the recipe you plan to make. Then, check to make sure you have all of the ingredients.

Clear a nice large workspace on the kitchen counter or table. Be sure to wipe off your workspace with a clean wet sponge or cloth.

Put all the ingredients and tools in your workspace.

Follow the recipe's steps in order.

Clean up spills right away.

Clean up the kitchen so you'll be allowed to use it again!

Have fun!

RED HOT SAFETY TIPS

For each recipe in this book you will need to use either the oven, stove, or toaster oven. *Always ask an adult for permission to use these appliances.* You may also want to ask an adult to help you use these appliances safely.

When you use the oven, stove, or toaster oven, it's important to remember the following:

 Keep a fire extinguisher handy.

 Use pot holders or oven mitts to put pizzas in and take pizzas out of the oven.

 Use a timer when baking pizza in the oven or toaster oven. Check pizza about 5 minutes before timer goes off to make sure it's not burning. Remove pizza if it looks like it is done or if it is burning.

 Put a hot pizza pan on the stove or wooden cutting board. Never put a hot pan on the counter.

 Let pizzas cool before eating. Hot cheese can burn you, so don't touch or eat pizza before you're sure it's cool enough.

 Turn off the oven, stove, or toaster oven after you're finished using it.

PIZZABIT

Did you know that if you lined up all the pizza that Americans eat every day it would stretch across 100 football fields? That's a lot of pie!

PIZZA POTS AND PANS

Before you begin any baking project, make sure you have all the right ingredients and the right tools. The following list of pots, pans, bowls, spoons, graters, and more will teach you a bit about some of the tools you'll need to make your favorite pizza pie. Be sure all tools are washed and dried thoroughly before beginning any pizza baking project.

Cheese Grater — Use a grater to shred cheese and vegetables for pizza toppings. *(See page 38 for illustrated technique.)*

Cutting Board — Use a cutting board when you cut fruits or vegetables. Be sure to wash it thoroughly when you're done.

Measuring Cups and Spoons — Use clearly labeled measuring cups and spoons so that you're sure you're measuring things correctly.

Metal Spatula — You'll need a metal spatula for removing Peewee Pizzas from the toaster oven. A metal spatula is also good for taking baked goods off cookie sheets.

Mixing Bowls — You'll need a very large mixing bowl to make pizza dough. Use a smaller mixing bowl to mix together pizza toppings.

Pizza Cutter — A pizza cutter is the best tool for cutting a pizza. If you don't have a pizza cutter, ask an adult to help you with a sharp knife.

Pizza Pans — The recipes in this book call for a 12-inch pizza pan. You can also use a cookie sheet, a cake pan, or a larger pizza pan (if you increase the recipe). Be sure to use a metal pan.

Plastic Bags — You'll need a large plastic bag the size of a bread bag for storing dough while it rises. You'll need a smaller, thicker plastic bag, such as a zipper bag, for smashing garlic and tomatoes.

Pot Holders or Oven Mitts — Use either pot holders or oven mitts to remove hot things from the oven and toaster oven.

Pots — You'll need a heavy-bottomed, 3-quart pot with a lid to make Super Snappy Pizza Sauce.

Rolling Pin — You'll need a rolling pin to roll your dough into a circle large enough to fit a pizza pan. (*See page 27 for illustrated technique.*) If you don't have a rolling pin, try using a clean metal can or a large, clean glass jar.

Rubber Spatula — A rubber spatula is good for scraping out bowls and spreading toppings on pizzas.

Spoons — You'll need a large wooden spoon, a large metal spoon, and a small cereal spoon. Always use a wooden spoon to stir hot things on the stove.

Table Knife — A table knife is what you use at the dinner table. It's not very sharp, but it's good for cutting a lot of things.

Timer — Always use a timer when baking pizzas.

PEEWEE PIZZAS

Peewee Pizzas are mini pies which you cook in the toaster oven instead of the oven. They're perfect for after school snacks. Best of all, they are quick, safe, and easy to make — so you can have pizza anytime!

MAKES 2
PEEWEE PIES

PREHEAT TOASTER
OVEN TO BROIL

INGREDIENTS
ENGLISH MUFFIN
2 TABLESPOONS
   SPAGHETTI OR
   PIZZA SAUCE
4 TABLESPOONS GRAT-
   ED MOZZARELLA
   (SEE PAGE 38 FOR
   ILLUSTRATED
   TECHNIQUE)

TOOLS
TABLE KNIFE
MEASURING SPOONS
GRATER
POT HOLDERS
METAL SPATULA

TRADITIONAL PEEWEE PIE

A Peewee Pizza Classic!

1. Use table knife to split **English muffin** in two.

2. Put **1 tablespoon sauce** on each muffin half.

3. Sprinkle **2 tablespoons mozzarella** on each muffin half.

4. Bake in toaster oven for **3–5 minutes,** until cheese bubbles. Use pot holders and metal spatula to remove from toaster oven. *Turn off toaster oven.*

5. Buon Apetito! Start thinking now of toppings to put on your next Peewee Pie.

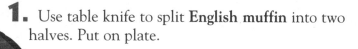

ENGLISH MUFFIN MORNING PIES
Pizza for breakfast!

MAKES 2
MORNING PIES

PREHEAT TOASTER
OVEN TO BROIL

1. Use table knife to split **English muffin** into two halves. Put on plate.

2. Carefully crack **egg** on edge of small bowl. Pour egg into bowl, being careful not to get any shell in the bowl. Beat egg with fork until egg is all yellow.

3. Add **Cheddar cheese** to egg. Mix well.

4. Carefully spoon **egg mixture** bit by bit onto muffin halves. Put equal amount on each muffin half. Be sure to let egg soak into muffin before adding more so that egg doesn't spill over. Carefully wash any dripped egg off plate.

5. Heat in toaster oven for *3–5 minutes* until puffy and lightly browned. **Watch carefully.**

6. Use pot holders and spatula to remove muffins from toaster oven. Put on plate. *Turn off toaster oven.*

7. Spread **1 teaspoon sauce** onto each muffin half.

8. What a great way to wake up in the morning!

INGREDIENTS
1 ENGLISH MUFFIN
1 EGG
2 TABLESPOONS
    GRATED CHEDDAR
    (SEE PAGE 38 FOR
    ILLUSTRATED
    TECHNIQUE)
2 TEASPOONS PIZZA
    SAUCE

TOOLS
TABLE KNIFE
PLATE
SMALL BOWL
FORK
GRATER
MEASURING SPOONS
POT HOLDERS
METAL SPATULA

MAKES 3
CRACKER PIES

PREHEAT TOASTER
OVEN TO BROIL

INGREDIENTS 1
1 CRACKER (USE YOUR
FAVORITE KIND)
1 TEASPOON PIZZA
SAUCE
1 TEASPOON GRATED
MOZZARELLA
(SEE PAGE 38 FOR
ILLUSTRATED
TECHNIQUE)

INGREDIENTS 2
1 CRACKER
1 PIECE PEPPERONI
1 SKINNY SLICE
CHEDDAR CHEESE

INGREDIENTS 3
1 CRACKER
1 TEASPOON PIZZA
SAUCE
1 TEASPOON
PARMESAN CHEESE

TOOLS
MEASURING SPOONS
GRATER
POT HOLDERS
METAL SPATULA

CRISPY-CRUNCHY CRACKER PIES

Here are three great ways to make your cracker pies.
Use your imagination to come up with other tasty combinations.

1. Assemble **ingredients** (in the order given) on top of **crackers.**

2. Heat for *1 minute* in toaster oven. **Watch carefully**, these burn easily!

3. Use pot holders and spatula to remove from toaster oven.
Turn off toaster oven.

4. Let cool and then start crunching and munching!

PRIMO PITA PIZZA PIE

A miniature gourmet pizza pie!

PREHEAT TOASTER OVEN TO BROIL

1. Put **tomatoes** into plastic bag. Squeeze air out of bag. Close bag tightly. Use your hands to smash and squish until tomatoes are well squished.

2. Dump **squished tomatoes** onto **pita bread.** Spread over bread.

3. If **olives** have pits, gently squish each olive between your fingers until pit pops out. Throw away pits. Put olives on cutting board and cut into small pieces. Arrange evenly on top of pita.

4. Sprinkle **parmesan** and **mozzarella** evenly over pita.

5. Sprinkle on **black pepper, garlic powder,** and **oregano.**

6. Heat in toaster oven for **3–5 minutes,** or until cheese is melted and bubbly. Watch carefully!

7. Use spatula and pot holders to remove from toaster oven. *Turn off toaster oven.*

8. Presto! Your Primo Pita Pizza Pie!

INGREDIENTS
4 CHERRY TOMATOES
1 PITA BREAD
4 BLACK OLIVES
1 TEASPOON PARMESAN CHEESE
2 TABLESPOONS GRATED MOZZARELLA (SEE PAGE 38 FOR ILLUSTRATED TECHNIQUE)
SPRINKLE OF BLACK PEPPER
PINCH OF GARLIC POWDER
PINCH OF OREGANO

TOOLS
SMALL, CLEAN, STURDY PLASTIC BAG (A ZIPPER BAG IS PERFECT)
TABLE KNIFE
CUTTING BOARD
GRATER
MEASURING SPOONS
SPATULA
POT HOLDERS

Tomatoes are very popular in Italy. They are called pomodoro, which means apple of gold.

9

MAKES 1
PIZZA-RITO

PREHEAT TOASTER
OVEN TO 325°F

INGREDIENTS
1 SOFT TORTILLA
1 TABLESPOON PIZZA
  SAUCE OR SALSA
1 TEASPOON
  PARMESAN CHEESE
2 TABLESPOONS GRAT-
  ED MOZZARELLA
  (SEE PAGE 38 FOR
  ILLUSTRATED
  TECHNIQUE)

TOOLS
MEASURING SPOONS
SPOON
GRATER
POT HOLDERS
METAL SPATULA

PIZZA-RITO
A burrito goes to Italy!

 Use spoon to spread **sauce** or **salsa** evenly over **tortilla**.

 Sprinkle **parmesan** and **mozzarella** cheeses evenly over tortilla.

 Roll up tortilla. Use your hands to gently flatten so that tortilla stays closed.

 Bake in toaster oven for **5 minutes.** Use pot holders and metal spatula to remove from toaster oven. Let cool. *Turn off oven.*

 Say Pizza-Rito five times fast.

 PIZZABIT

Tortillas come from Mexico. Traditionally they were made from just cornmeal and water. The cornmeal-water mixture was rolled and patted into a flat pancake and cooked on a hot clay or metal griddle. Many cooks in Mexico still make tortillas in this old traditional way.

TASTY TOSTADA PIE

A pizza goes to Mexico!

1. Use table knife to spread **sauce** or **salsa** evenly over **tostada**.

2. Sprinkle **black beans** and **corn** evenly over tostada.

3. Sprinkle **mozzarella** evenly over tostada.

4. Heat in toaster oven for *3–5 minutes.* **Watch carefully,** this will burn easily! Remove with pot holders and metal spatula. *Turn off toaster oven.*

5. Crunch!

 MAKES 1 PIE

PREHEAT TOASTER OVEN TO 325°F

INGREDIENTS
1 TOSTADA (FLAT TACO SHELL)
1 TABLESPOON PIZZA SAUCE OR SALSA
1 TABLESPOON BLACK BEANS
1 TABLESPOON FROZEN OR CANNED CORN
1 TABLESPOON GRATED MOZZARELLA (SEE PAGE 38 FOR ILLUSTRATED TECHNIQUE)

TOOLS
TABLE KNIFE
GRATER
POT HOLDERS
METAL SPATULA

 MAKES 2 PIES

PREHEAT TOASTER OVEN TO 325°F

INGREDIENTS
1 WHOLE PITA BREAD
2 TABLESPOONS RICOTTA CHEESE
2 TABLESPOONS GRATED MOZZARELLA CHEESE (SEE PAGE 38 FOR ILLUSTRATED TECHNIQUE)
4 CHERRY TOMATOES
2 TABLESPOONS FROZEN OR CANNED CORN OR 6 PIECES SLICED PEPPERONI

TOOLS
TABLE KNIFE
MEASURING SPOONS
GRATER
CUTTING BOARD
SPOON
POT HOLDERS
METAL SPATULA

CRAM-JAMMED PITA PIES
Pitas crammed with delicious pizza stuff.

 Use table knife to cut **pita bread** in half. You should have 2 pita pockets.

 Put **1 tablespoon of ricotta** into each pita pocket. Use knife to scrape ricotta from measuring spoon. Gently spread ricotta on inside of pita pockets.

 Put **1 tablespoon of grated mozzarella** into each pita pocket.

 Put **cherry tomatoes** on cutting board. Stick knife into the top of a tomato. Pull out knife and cut tomato in half where you made cut. Cut tomatoes into small pieces.

PIZZABIT

No one in Europe had even heard of tomatoes until the 16th Century when explorers brought them back from South America. And it took a long time before tomatoes were ever used in food! Most Europeans thought that they were poisonous and used them only as ornamental house plants.

5 Spoon equal amount of **chopped tomatoes** into each pita pocket.

6 Put **1 tablespoon of corn** *or* **3 pieces of pepperoni** into each pita pocket.

7 Bake for **5–7 minutes** in toaster oven. Use pot holders and metal spatula to remove from toaster oven. *Turn off toaster oven.* Let pies cool.

8 Jam a Cram-Jammed Pita Pie right into your mouth.

MAKES 2 ZAGELS

PREHEAT TOASTER
OVEN TO BROIL

INGREDIENTS
1 BAGEL
2 TABLESPOONS PIZZA
SAUCE
2 TABLESPOONS GRAT-
ED MOZZARELLA
(SEE PAGE 38 FOR
ILLUSTRATED
TECHNIQUE)
2 TEASPOONS
PARMESAN CHEESE

TOOLS
TABLE KNIFE
SMALL SPOON
CEREAL BOWL
GRATER
MEASURING SPOONS
POT HOLDERS
METAL SPATULA

ZAGELS
Pizza in a Bagel.

 Cut **bagel** in half to make two circles. (You may want to ask an adult to do this with a sharp knife.)

 Use spoon to scoop out a "ditch" or "moat" in each bagel half. (*See page 16 for illustrated technique.*) Put **bagel crumbs** in cereal bowl.

 Add **sauce, mozzarella,** and **parmesan cheese** to cereal bowl. Mix well.

 Use spoon or your fingers to stuff **bagel-sauce** mixture back into bagel. Put an equal amount in each bagel half.

 PIZZABIT

Did you ever wonder what gives bagels their shine? Water! Before bagels are baked, they are boiled or "kettled" in water.

Heat in toaster oven for **3 minutes,** or until lightly browned.
Remove with pot holders and metal spatula. *Turn off toaster oven.*

A bagel never tasted this good!

HOW TO SCOOP OUT A BAGEL

1. Hold bagel upright with one hand, and use a knife to "saw" bagel in half. Cut bagel into two circles.

2. Put bagel circles on flat surface such as the counter or cutting board.

3. Use a small spoon with a pointed tip to scoop out the bagel. Gently push the spoon into the bagel. Next, scoop out a piece of bagel. Don't scoop too close to the edge or you'll break the bagel.

4. Keep scooping out pieces of bagel until you've made a "ditch" or "moat" all the way around the bagel. Make the ditch as deep as you want.

5. Stuff the bagel with anything you like.

LOADS OF DOUGH

Making dough has got to be the best part of making pizza. Dough is fun.
You can knead it, punch it, roll it, stretch it, pull it, and even tie it in knots!
This chapter gives you recipes for both yeast-risen and quick doughs.
Try them all and decide which ones you like best.

MAKES ENOUGH
FOR ONE 12-INCH
PIE

INGREDIENTS
2 TEASPOONS ACTIVE
 DRY YEAST
¾ CUP VERY WARM
 WATER
2 TEASPOONS SUGAR
1 TABLESPOON OIL
1 TEASPOON SALT
¼ CUP CORNMEAL
1 TEASPOON OIL
2–2½ CUPS WHITE
 FLOUR + EXTRA TO
 SPRINKLE ON
 HANDS, DOUGH,
 AND WORK SPACE

TOOLS
MEASURING CUPS
 AND SPOONS
SMALL BOWL
SMALL SPOON
LARGE MIXING BOWL
LARGE WOODEN
 SPOON
CLEAN FLOURED
 SURFACE
LARGE, CLEAN PLASTIC
 BAG (A BREAD BAG
 IS PERFECT)
TWIST-TIE

DIVINE DOUGH
Divine dough for a divine pie!

 Put the **yeast, water,** and **sugar** into small bowl. Mix well. Let sit for **5 minutes** — until the top looks foamy.

 Add **1 tablespoon oil** and the **salt** to **yeast mixture.** Stir well. Pour into large bowl.

 Add **cornmeal** to the bowl. Next add **flour, 1 cup at a time.** Use wooden spoon to stir well after each addition. Use your hands when dough is too hard to stir. Add flour, a little at a time, until dough is no longer sticky.

 Put **dough** onto a clean floured surface. Knead the dough. *(See page 20 for illustrated technique.)* Knead dough until it is smooth, shiny, and stretchy. Sprinkle with flour to keep it from sticking.

 Put **1 teaspoon of oil** into plastic bag. Squish the bag between your hands until the inside is well oiled.

 Form dough into a ball and put into bag. Twist bag tightly to get the air out. Use a twist-tie to close the *top* of the bag. Be sure to leave enough space in the bag to let dough double in size.

 Put dough in a warm (not hot) place. Let rise for about **1 hour.** The dough should double in size.

Open bag and turn it upside down to dump dough onto floured surface. Make two fists and punch down dough. Knead for **1 minute.**

Stretch, pull, and roll your Divine Dough in any shape you want. *(See page 27 to learn how to roll out dough to fit pizza pan.)*

PIZZABIT

When you add sugar to the yeast and warm water in this recipe, you are actually feeding the yeast! The yeast "eats" the sugar. When you add this yeast mixture to the flour, the yeast eats the flour's natural sugars. As it eats, the yeast produces gas. This gas "inflates" the dough, causing it to rise.

HOW TO KNEAD DOUGH

1. Sprinkle flour onto a clean counter top or table top. Keep a cup of flour close by to sprinkle counter with more if the dough becomes sticky.

2. Form dough into a ball.

3. Put dough ball onto floured surface. Lightly dust your hands with flour.

4. Knead the dough. Use the heels of your hands (the part closest to your wrist) to push the dough out and away from you. Make the dough longer.

5. Grab dough with your fingers and fold it back towards you.

6. Turn dough clockwise, about one-quarter of a circle.

7. Repeat process. Push dough out with the heels of your hands. Grab with your fingers to fold dough in half. Turn dough. Push, fold, turn...

8. To keep dough from sticking, sprinkle flour on your hands, counter, and dough. You'll probably need to do this a few times while kneading.

9. Knead dough for as long as you can — 5–10 minutes is best. Your dough will turn from a shaggy mess into a smooth, elastic ball.

DYNAMO DOUGH

Dynamo dough is dynamite stuff!

MAKES ENOUGH
FOR ONE 12-INCH
PIE

1 Put **yeast, water,** and **honey** into the small bowl. Mix well. Let sit for **5 minutes** — until the top of the water looks foamy.

2 Add **1 tablespoon oil** and the **salt** to **yeast mixture**. Stir well. Pour into the large bowl.

INGREDIENTS

2 TEASPOONS ACTIVE
   DRY YEAST
¾ CUP VERY WARM
   WATER
2 TEASPOONS HONEY
1 TABLESPOON OIL
1 TEASPOON SALT
¼ CUP WHEAT GERM
1 CUP WHITE FLOUR
1½ CUPS WHOLE
   WHEAT FLOUR +
   EXTRA TO SPRIN-
   KLE ON HANDS,
   DOUGH, AND
   WORK SPACE
1 TEASPOON OIL

TOOLS

MEASURING CUPS
   AND SPOONS
SMALL BOWL
SMALL SPOON
LARGE MIXING BOWL
LARGE WOODEN
   SPOON
CLEAN, FLOURED
   SURFACE
LARGE CLEAN PLASTIC
   BAG (A BREAD BAG
   IS PERFECT)
TWIST-TIE

21

Add **wheat germ** to bowl. Next, add **white and whole wheat flour** to bowl, **1 cup at a time**. Use wooden spoon to stir well after each addition. Mix with your hands when dough is too hard to stir. Add flour, a little at a time, until dough is no longer sticky.

 Put **dough** onto a clean floured surface. Knead dough. *(See page 20 for illustrated technique.)* Knead dough until it is smooth, shiny, and stretchy. Sprinkle with flour to keep it from sticking.

Put **1 teaspoon of oil** into plastic bag. Squish the bag between your hands until the inside is well oiled.

Form dough into a ball and put into bag. Twist bag tightly to get all the air out. Use a twist-tie to close the *top* of the bag. Be sure to leave enough space in the bag to let the dough double in size.

Put dough in a warm, not hot, place. Let rise for about **1 hour.** The dough should double in size.

Open bag and turn it upside down to dump dough onto floured surface. Make two fists and punch down dough. Knead for **1 minute.**

Stretch, pull, and roll your Dynamo Dough into any shape you want! *(See page 27 to learn how to roll out dough to fit pizza pan.)*

MAKES ENOUGH
FOR ONE 12-INCH
SWEETIE PIE

INGREDIENTS

2 TEASPOONS ACTIVE
    DRY YEAST
½ CUP VERY WARM
    WATER
3 TABLESPOONS
    SUGAR
1 TABLESPOON OIL
1 TEASPOON SALT
½ CUP MILK
2½–3 CUPS FLOUR +
    EXTRA TO SPRIN-
    KLE ON HANDS,
    DOUGH, AND
    WORK SPACE
1 TEASPOON OIL

TOOLS

MEASURING CUPS
    AND SPOONS
SMALL BOWL
SMALL SPOON
LARGE MIXING BOWL
WOODEN SPOON
CLEAN, FLOURED
    SURFACE
LARGE, CLEAN PLASTIC
    BAG (A BREAD BAG
    IS PERFECT)
TWIST-TIE

SWEETIE PIE DOUGH

Sweetie Pie Dough for your favorite sweetie pie!

1. Put **yeast, water,** and **sugar** into small bowl. Mix well. Let sit for **5 minutes** — until the top of the water looks foamy.

2. Add **1 tablespoon oil** and the **salt** to **yeast mixture.** Stir well. Pour into the large mixing bowl.

3. Add **milk.**

4. Add **flour, 1 cup at a time.** Use wooden spoon to stir well after each addition. When dough gets too hard to stir, use your clean hands to mix it. Continue to add flour, a little at a time, until dough is no longer sticky.

5. Put the dough onto a clean floured surface. Knead dough. (*See page 20 for illustrated technique.*) Knead dough until it is smooth, shiny, and stretchy. Sprinkle with flour to keep the dough from sticking.

6. Put **1 teaspoon of oil** into plastic bag. Squish the bag between your hands until inside is well oiled.

7. Form the dough into a ball and put into bag. Twist bag tightly to get all the air out. Use a twist-tie to close the *top* of the bag. Be sure to leave enough space in the bag to let the dough double in size.

8. Put dough in a warm, (not hot), place. Let rise for about **1 hour.** The dough should double in size.

9. Open bag and turn it upside down to remove dough. Make two fists and punch down dough. Knead for *1 minute*.

10. Stretch, pull, and roll your Sweetie Pie Dough into any shape you want! *(See page 27 to learn how to roll out dough to fit a pizza pan.)*

MAKES ENOUGH
FOR ONE 12-INCH
PIE

INGREDIENTS
2¼ CUPS WHITE OR
    WHOLE WHEAT
    FLOUR + EXTRA TO
    SPRINKLE ON
    HANDS, DOUGH,
    AND WORK SPACE
2 TEASPOONS SUGAR
1 TEASPOON SALT
1 TEASPOON BAKING
    POWDER
⅔ CUP MILK
¼ CUP OIL

TOOLS
MEASURING CUPS
    AND SPOONS
LARGE BOWL
LARGE WOODEN
    SPOON
CLEAN, FLOURED
    SURFACE

NIFTY JIFFY DOUGH

Great dough for a super quick pizza.

1. Put **flour, sugar, salt,** and **baking powder** into the large bowl. Use wooden spoon to mix well.

2. Pour **milk** and **oil** into **flour mixture.** Use spoon or your hands to mix well.

3. Form **dough** into a ball. Put onto clean floured surface. Knead for **1–2 minutes**. *(See page 20 for illustrated technique.)* Sprinkle with flour to keep dough from sticking.

4. Roll, stretch, and shape dough for recipe of your choice. *(See page 27 to learn how to roll out dough to fit pizza pan.)*

5. Phew! That was fast!

PIZZABIT

In addition to flour, water, and yeast, all bread contains gluten. Gluten is the stuff that keeps bread from falling apart. You form gluten whenever you knead any flour and water mixture into a smooth, shiny ball.

As dough rises, the gluten stretches and traps the gases released from the yeast. This turns the dough ball into a "dough balloon." If it weren't for gluten, all baked dough would be as flat as a cracker!

HOW TO ROLL AND STRETCH DOUGH TO FIT A PIZZA PAN

 Prepare pizza pan. Grease pan lightly with oil. Sprinkle with cornmeal. (Cornmeal helps cooked pizza slide off pan easily.)

 Sprinkle flour onto a clean counter top or table top. Keep a cup of flour close by to sprinkle on dough when it gets sticky.

 Put dough onto floured surface. If your dough contains yeast, punch dough down to get out the extra gas.

 Knead dough for 1 minute. (*See page 20 for illustrated technique.*)

 Use your hands to flatten dough into a circle.

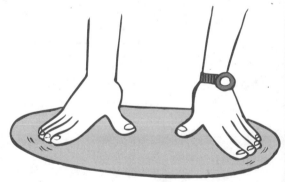

6 Stretch out dough with your hands and fingers. This will make it easier to roll with a rolling pin.

7 Use a rolling pin to roll dough into a large circle. Roll from the center of the circle out to the edge. Roll in each direction to keep an even circle.

8 Carefully pick up dough circle and turn it about one-quarter of a circle. Sprinkle flour underneath and on top of dough if it is sticky.

9 Repeat the process. Roll dough. Turn dough. Roll dough. Roll out dough until you make a circle as big or almost as big as your pizza pan.

 Carefully fold dough in half and place on pizza pan. Unfold dough and fit evenly in pan.

 Use your hands to pull and stretch dough to make it as big as the pizza pan. This will be easier if you let dough sit in the pan for a few minutes before stretching it. You can fix any holes you make in the dough by pinching the dough together at the hole.

 Pinch an edge around the circle.

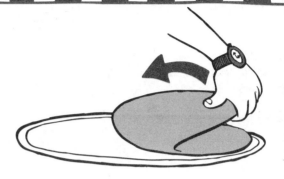

DOUGH ROLLING TIPS

1. Use less dough for a thinner crust, more dough for a thicker crust.

2. If you are using a square or rectangular pan, roll dough into a square or a rectangle instead of a circle.

3. For individual pies, divide dough into 3 or 4 pieces. Roll each piece of dough into a small circle. Place on cookie sheet.

MAKES ENOUGH
FOR ONE 12-INCH
PIE

INGREDIENTS
½ CUP GRATED
   MOZZARELLA
   (SEE PAGE 38 FOR
   ILLUSTRATED
   TECHNIQUE)
½ CUP GRATED
   PARMESAN CHEESE
1 RECIPE DOUGH

TOOLS
GRATER
MEASURING CUPS
SMALL BOWL
SPOON
CLEAN, FLOURED
   SURFACE

EASY CHEESY DOUGH

Like cheese? Try this tasty dough to add extra cheese to your favorite pie.

1. Put **mozzarella** and **parmesan** in small bowl. Mix well.

2. Put **dough** onto clean, floured surface. Punch down and flatten into circle.

3. Pour ¼ **cup cheese mixture** onto dough. Next, knead dough until cheese is mixed in. Repeat until you've mixed all of the cheese into the dough.

4. Roll, stretch or pull in any shape you like. *(See page 27 to learn how to roll dough to fit pizza pan.)*

5. Easy Cheesy Dough is great without any toppings! To try it, bake at 400°F for **15 minutes**.

WHOPPING TOPPINGS

Top your pizza with Whopping Toppings and you'll have a
whopping good pizza pie! In this chapter you'll find recipes for
both very traditional and very unusual 12-inch pizza pies. All
of them are delicious — so don't be shy to try!

Feel free to make substitutions if you don't have an ingredient, or if you're sure you don't like
an ingredient. And, of course, you can always top your pizza with more or less of any of the
toppings. (*See page 79 for more topping ideas.*)

MAKES 4½ CUPS
SAUCE

INGREDIENTS
4 CLOVES GARLIC
1 28-OUNCE
 CAN CRUSHED
 TOMATOES
2 6-OUNCE CANS
 TOMATO PASTE
1 TABLESPOON OIL
2 TEASPOONS DRIED
 BASIL
2 TEASPOONS DRIED
 OREGANO
1 TEASPOON SALT
¾ CUP WATER

TOOLS
SMALL JUICE GLASS
SMALL, CLEAN,
 STURDY PLASTIC
 BAG (A ZIPPER BAG
 IS PERFECT)
CUTTING BOARD
ROLLING PIN
MEASURING SPOONS
 AND CUPS
CAN OPENER
HEAVY-BOTTOMED
 3-QUART POT
 WITH LID
SMALL SPOON
LARGE WOODEN
 SPOON
OVEN MITTS

— SUPER SNAPPY PIZZA SAUCE —

Make this sauce ahead of time so you'll have it ready for pizza anytime!

1. Use bottom of juice glass to gently crush each **garlic clove**. Peel skin off the garlic cloves.

2. Do the Garlic Smash. Put garlic cloves into small bag. Use rolling pin to pound and smash garlic until it is well smashed. (*See page 34 for illustrated technique.*)

3. Use a can opener to open **crushed tomatoes** and **tomato paste**. Set aside.

4. Put **oil** and **smashed garlic** into pot. Heat on stove at medium heat for **1 minute.** Stir constantly with wooden spoon. *Turn off heat.*

5. Use a spoon to remove **tomato paste** from can and add it and **tomatoes** to the pot. Stir well.

6. Add **basil, oregano, salt,** and **water** to pot. Stir well.

7. Turn stove back on. Cook sauce partially covered over medium-low heat for about **1 hour. Watch carefully,**

If you can't use your Super Snappy Pizza Sauce right away, put the cooled sauce in a jar or plastic container and store in refrigerator. Refrigerated sauce will keep for a week or more. You may also freeze the sauce for up to six months.

Be sure to wear an oven mitt. Stir often so sauce doesn't burn. Add water if sauce looks like it might burn. When **1 hour** is up, *turn the stove off*. Let sauce cool.

8. Perfecto!

HOW TO DO THE GARLIC SMASH

1. Use the bottom of a juice glass to gently crush the clove of garlic.

2. Peel the dry, crackly skin off of the garlic clove.

3. Put garlic into a small sturdy plastic bag. A zipper bag is perfect. Partially seal bag. Leave a small opening for air to escape out as you do the smash. If you don't have a plastic bag, wrap garlic in aluminum foil. Put garlic on cutting board.

4. Use a rolling pin to pound and smash garlic. Do this until garlic is well smashed.

5. Add smashed garlic to your favorite recipe.

RED HOT SIZZLING SALSA

Warning: This salsa is only for kids with extra tough tongues!

MAKES 4 CUPS SALSA

1. Use a can opener to open **crushed tomatoes** and **tomato paste.** Pour into mixing bowl. Mix well. (Use a small spoon to get all the tomato paste out of can.)

2. Peel **onion.** Be sure to remove all of the dry, crackly outer skin. Next, use table knife or your fingers to peel off two or three layers of onion. (*See page 36 for illustrated technique.*)

3. Break or cut **onion layers** into very small pieces. Add to tomato mixture.

4. Add **garlic powder, salt,** and **crushed red pepper** to tomato mixture. Mix well.

5. Hot-cha-cha!

PIZZABIT

Do onions make you cry? Yes? That's not surprising. When you chop an onion you release a gas which forms sulfuric acid when it meets your eyes. Ouch! The only way to avoid this pain is to get used to it by chopping lots and lots of onions. Or, wear safety goggles when you chop.

INGREDIENTS
1 28-OUNCE CAN CRUSHED TOMATOES
1 6-OUNCE CAN TOMATO PASTE
1 ONION
½ TEASPOON GARLIC POWDER
½ TEASPOON SALT
¼ TEASPOON CRUSHED HOT RED PEPPER (USE MORE OR LESS PEPPER TO YOUR TASTE)

TOOLS
CAN OPENER
MIXING BOWL
LARGE AND SMALL SPOONS
TABLE KNIFE
CUTTING BOARD
MEASURING SPOONS

HOW TO DO THE ONION PEEL

1. Peel all of the dry, crackly skin off of the onion.

2. Use your fingers or the table knife to pull off layers of the onion one at a time.

3. Put onion layers on cutting board and cut into small pieces.

4. Add onion pieces to your favorite recipe.

PIZZERIA PIE

Just your usual old super delicious pizzeria-style pizza.

 1' Pour **sauce** on **dough.** Use table knife to spread evenly over dough.

 2' Sprinkle **mozzarella cheese** evenly over dough.

 3' Bake in oven for **20 minutes.** Use pot holders to remove from oven. *Turn off oven.*

 4' Say "Pizzeria Pie" seven times fast.

PIZZABIT

Back in 1889 Italian Queen Margherita and her husband King Umberto I took a trip to Naples, the birthplace of pizza. Poor Margherita had never had pizza before, and she really wanted to try it. But, because she was a queen, she was not allowed to visit the local pizzeria. So, she invited the great pizza chef Don Raffaele Esposito to the palace where she was staying and asked him to make her a pizza.

Don Raffaele made many different kinds of pizza for Margherita. Her favorite was one made from tomatoes, mozzarella cheese, and basil. Don Raffaele named it Pizza Margherita, and it quickly became very popular throughout the land. America's favorite cheese pizza is a lot like Pizza Margherita.

 MAKES ONE 12-INCH PIZZA

PREHEAT OVEN TO 400°F

INGREDIENTS
1 RECIPE PREPARED PIZZA DOUGH PLACED ON GREASED PIZZA PAN
½ CUP PIZZA SAUCE
1 CUP GRATED MOZZARELLA CHEESE (SEE PAGE 38 FOR ILLUSTRATED TECHNIQUE)

TOOLS
GREASED PIZZA PAN
MEASURING CUPS
GRATER
TABLE KNIFE
POT HOLDERS

HOW TO GRATE CHEESE

1. Start with a large hunk of chilled cheese.

2. If you are using an upright grater, place it in a bowl or on a cutting board. If you are using a flat grater, place it on top of a bowl.

3. Hold one end of the cheese with your fingers. Put the other end against the large holes of the grater.

4. Press hard and rub the cheese back and forth over grater. You should see the grated cheese fall into the bowl or on the cutting board.

5. Measure the cheese from time to time to see how much you've grated.

6. Grate the cheese until you have enough for your favorite recipe. Wrap up the remaining cheese and refrigerate until it's pizza time again!

7. Use this same method to grate carrots and other vegetables and fruits.

IMPORTANT NOTE

Be sure to keep your fingers and knuckles away from the grater. If the cheese or vegetable you are grating becomes too small to grate, just cut or break it into small pieces. (Or, just pop it in your mouth!)

BIG RED POLKA DOT PIE

Just another name for everyone's favorite pepperoni pie.

1. Pour **sauce** onto **dough.** Use table knife to spread evenly over dough.

2. Sprinkle **mozzarella** evenly over pizza.

3. Arrange **pepperoni slices** evenly over pizza.

4. Bake for **20 minutes.** Use pot holders to remove from oven. *Turn off oven.*

5. Be sure to wear polka dots while you eat your Big Red Polka Dot Pie!

MAKES ONE
12-INCH PIE

PREHEAT OVEN
TO 400°F

INGREDIENTS
1 RECIPE PREPARED
   PIZZA DOUGH
   PLACED ON
   GREASED PIZZA
   PAN
½ CUP PIZZA SAUCE
1 CUP GRATED MOZ-
   ZARELLA (SEE
   PAGE 38 FOR
   ILLUSTRATED
   TECHNIQUE)
15 SLICES PEPPERONI

TOOLS
GREASED PIZZA PAN
MEASURING CUPS
GRATER
TABLE KNIFE
POT HOLDERS

This one's only for real hams.

INGREDIENTS (left sidebar)

MAKES ONE
12-INCH PIE

PREHEAT OVEN
TO 400°F

INGREDIENTS

1 RECIPE PREPARED
PIZZA DOUGH
PLACED ON
GREASED PIZZA
PAN
½ CUP PIZZA SAUCE
1 CUP GRATED MOZ-
ZARELLA CHEESE
(SEE PAGE 38 FOR
ILLUSTRATED
TECHNIQUE)
4 PIECES DELI-SLICED
HAM

TOOLS

GREASED PIZZA PAN
MEASURING CUPS
GRATER
TABLE KNIFE
POT HOLDERS

Instructions

1. Pour **sauce** onto **dough.** Use table knife to spread evenly over dough.

2. Sprinkle **mozzarella** evenly over pizza.

3. Break **ham** into small pieces. Sprinkle evenly over pizza.

4. Bake in oven for **20 minutes.** Use pot holders to remove from oven. *Turn off oven.*

5. Be sure to ham it up while you eat your Ham It Up Pie.

PIZZABIT

One of the very first pizzerias was called Porta Alba. It was in Naples, Italy, the birthplace of pizza. This pizzeria was lucky to have a very smart pizza chef. He knew that a great pizza needed to be baked in a very hot oven. So, he lined his oven with the hottest rock he could think of — volcanic lava! The lava helped retain the heat and keep the oven hot. Today many pizza ovens in Italy are lined with lava — and they are very, very hot.

CANADIAN BACON AND CHEDDAR PIE

This pizza is wonderful on a cold winter night.

1. Pour **sauce** on **dough.** Use table knife to spread evenly over dough.

2. Sprinkle **cheddar** and **mozzarella** evenly over pizza.

3. Break **Canadian bacon** into small pieces. Sprinkle evenly over pizza.

4. Bake in oven for **20 minutes.** Use pot holders to remove from oven. *Turn off oven.*

5. Delicious, eh?

 MAKES ONE 12-INCH PIE

PREHEAT OVEN TO 400°F

INGREDIENTS
1 RECIPE PREPARED PIZZA DOUGH PLACED ON GREASED PIZZA PAN
½ CUP PIZZA SAUCE
½ CUP GRATED CHEDDAR CHEESE (SEE PAGE 38 FOR ILLUSTRATED TECHNIQUE)
½ CUP GRATED MOZZARELLA
4 SLICES CANADIAN BACON

TOOLS
GREASED PIZZA PAN
MEASURING CUPS
GRATER
TABLE KNIFE
POT HOLDERS

 MAKES ONE
12-INCH PIE

PREHEAT OVEN
TO 400°F

INGREDIENTS
1 RECIPE PREPARED
    DOUGH IN PIZZA
    PAN
½ CUP PIZZA SAUCE
½ CUP RICOTTA
    CHEESE
2 TABLESPOONS GRAT-
    ED PARMESAN
    CHEESE (SEE
    PAGE 38 FOR
    ILLUSTRATED
    TECHNIQUE)
½ CUP GRATED
    MOZZARELLA
⅓ CUP CHOPPED
    FROZEN PEPPERS,
    THAWED
⅓ CUP CHOPPED
    FROZEN SPINACH,
    BROCCOLI, OR
    ZUCCHINI,
    THAWED

TOOLS
GREASED PIZZA PAN
MEASURING CUPS
    AND SPOONS
CEREAL BOWL
GRATER
SPOON
TABLE KNIFE
POT HOLDERS

GARDEN PARTY PIE
Great Grub!

 Put **sauce** and **ricotta** in cereal bowl. Stir well.

 Spoon **sauce-ricotta mixture** onto **dough.** Spread evenly over dough.

 Sprinkle **parmesan** and **mozzarella** evenly over pizza.

 Arrange **chopped pepper pieces** evenly on pizza.

 Arrange **spinach, broccoli,** or **zucchini** evenly on pizza.

 Bake for **20 minutes.** Remove with pot holders. *Turn off oven.*

PIZZABIT

Nineteenth Century Italians loved pizza so much that famous poets and artists wrote stories, poems, and songs about it!

7 Throw a Garden
Party Pizza Party!

PIPING PEPPERED PIE

Bet Peter Piper never had a piping peppered pie like this!

MAKES ONE 12-INCH PIE

PREHEAT OVEN TO 400°F

INGREDIENTS
1 RECIPE PREPARED PIZZA DOUGH PLACED ON PIZZA PAN
⅓ CUP PIZZA SAUCE OR SALSA
¼ CUP GRATED PARMESAN CHEESE
¾ CUP GRATED MOZZARELLA CHEESE (SEE PAGE 38 FOR ILLUSTRATED TECHNIQUE)
¾ CUP CHOPPED FROZEN RED AND GREEN PEPPERS, THAWED
SPRINKLE OF HOT RED PEPPER FLAKES (OPTIONAL)

TOOLS
GREASED PIZZA PAN
MEASURING CUPS
GRATER
TABLE KNIFE
POT HOLDERS

1. Pour **sauce** or **salsa** on dough. Use table knife to spread evenly over dough.

2. Sprinkle **parmesan** and **mozzarella** onto pizza. Be sure to cover pizza evenly with cheese.

3. Arrange **chopped pepper pieces** on pizza. Try to make designs or write words with the pepper pieces!

4. *Bake for 20 minutes.* Use pot holders to remove from oven. *Turn off oven.*

5. Pop a piece of Piping Peppered Pie into your mouth!

PEGASUS PIE
Food fit for the Gods!

1. Pour **sauce** onto **dough**. Use table knife to spread evenly over dough.

2. Carefully crack **egg** on edge of mixing bowl. Pour egg into bowl. Use fork to mix egg until all yellow.

3. Put **cottage cheese, feta cheese,** and **spinach** into bowl. Use spoon to mix well.

4. If **olives** have pits, gently squish them between your fingers. Remove the pits. Put olives on cutting board. Cut into small pieces.

5. Add **chopped olives** to **cheese-spinach mixture.** Mix well.

6. Spoon **cheese-spinach mixture** onto pizza. Spread evenly over dough.

7. Bake in oven for *20 minutes.* Use pot holders to remove from oven. *Turn off oven.*

8. Speak Greek while you eat your Pegasus Pie.

PIZZABIT

Pegasus is a winged flying horse from ancient Greek mythology. According to the myths, Pegasus loved to eat at the stables on Mount Olympus, the home of the Greek gods. Who knows — maybe his favorite dinner was Pegasus Pie!

MAKES ONE
12-INCH PIE

PREHEAT OVEN
TO 400°F

INGREDIENTS
1 RECIPE PREPARED
  PIZZA DOUGH
  PLACED ON
  GREASED PIZZA
  PAN
½ CUP PIZZA SAUCE
1 EGG
½ CUP COTTAGE
  CHEESE
½ CUP CRUMBLED
  FETA CHEESE
½ CUP CHOPPED
  FROZEN SPINACH,
  THAWED
8 BLACK OLIVES
  (OPTIONAL)

TOOLS
GREASED PIZZA PAN
MEASURING CUPS
  AND SPOONS
TABLE KNIFE
MIXING BOWL
FORK
LARGE SPOON
CUTTING BOARD
POT HOLDERS

MAKES ONE
12-INCH PIE

PREHEAT OVEN
TO 400°F

INGREDIENTS
1 RECIPE PREPARED
   PIZZA DOUGH
   PLACED ON
   GREASED PIZZA
   PAN
1 CUP MASHED
   POTATOES
⅓ CUP GRATED
   PARMESAN CHEESE
½ CUP RICOTTA
   CHEESE
1 CUP FROZEN OR
   CANNED CORN,
   THAWED
1 CLOVE GARLIC
¼ TEASPOON
   OREGANO

TOOLS
GREASED PIZZA PAN
MEASURING CUPS
   AND SPOONS
MIXING BOWL
LARGE SPOON
SMALL JUICE GLASS
SMALL, CLEAN,
   STURDY PLASTIC
   BAG (A ZIPPER BAG
   IS PERFECT)
ROLLING PIN
POT HOLDERS
CUTTING BOARD

SPUD-NUGGET PIE

Just another name for corn and mashed potato pie.

1. Put **mashed potatoes, parmesan cheese, ricotta cheese,** and **corn** into mixing bowl. Mix well.

2. Gently crush **garlic clove** with bottom of juice glass. Remove skin from garlic clove.

3. Do the Garlic Smash. Put **garlic clove** into plastic bag. Use end of rolling pin to smash garlic completely. (*See page 34 for illustrated technique.*)

4. Add **smashed garlic** to **potato-corn mixture.** Mix well.

5. Spoon **smashed garlic potato-corn mixture** onto pizza dough. Spread evenly over dough. Sprinkle with **oregano.**

6. Bake in oven for **15–20 minutes,** until lightly browned. Use pot holders to remove from oven. *Turn off oven.*

7. Say Spud-Nugget/Nud-Spugget seven times fast.

PIZZABIT

"Spud" is an all-time favorite nick-name for potato. It comes from the word spade — the tool that Eighteenth Century Irish potato farmers used to plant and dig their potatoes.

FIREBALL PIE

This is one hot pizza pie!

MAKES ONE
12-INCH PIE

PREHEAT OVEN
TO 400°F

 1 Pour **salsa** onto **dough.** Use table knife to spread evenly over dough.

 2 Bake in oven for **15 minutes.** Use pot holders to remove from oven. *Turn off oven.*

 3 If you're really brave, sprinkle this with red hot pepper flakes!

INGREDIENTS
1 RECIPE PREPARED
   EASY CHEESY
   DOUGH PLACED
   ON GREASED
   PIZZA PAN
½ CUP SALSA
RED HOT PEPPER
   FLAKES

TOOLS
GREASED PIZZA PAN
MEASURING CUP
TABLE KNIFE
POT HOLDERS

 PIZZABIT

Believe it or not, a red pepper is actually a green pepper — only older. The longer a pepper hangs on a vine, the more green color (chlorophyll) it loses. Once the green is gone, the pepper then shows off the red color which was hiding underneath the green all along. Because red peppers are riper than green peppers, they are also sweeter.

MAKES ONE
12-INCH PIE

PREHEAT OVEN
TO 400°F

INGREDIENTS
1 RECIPE PREPARED
PIZZA DOUGH
PLACED ON
GREASED PIZZA
PAN
2 CUPS COOKED
SPAGHETTI
¾ CUP PIZZA SAUCE
¼ CUP GRATED
PARMESAN CHEESE
½ CUP GRATED MOZ-
ZARELLA CHEESE
(SEE PAGE 38 FOR
ILLUSTRATED
TECHNIQUE)

TOOLS
GREASED PIZZA PAN
MEASURING CUPS
GRATER
MIXING BOWL
LARGE SPOON
POT HOLDERS

SPAGITZA
Spaghetti and pizza all in one!

1. Put **spaghetti, pizza sauce,** and **parmesan** into mixing bowl. Mix well.

2. Spoon **spaghetti-sauce mixture** onto **dough.** Use back of spoon (or your fingers, if you don't mind slippy-slimy noodles!) to spread mixture evenly over dough.

3. Sprinkle **mozzarella** evenly over pizza.

4. Bake for **20 minutes.** Use pot holders to remove from oven. *Turn off oven.*

5. Don't even think of slurping up these spaghetti noodles until they're cool.

NACHO CRUSH PIE

Serve this at your next fiesta.

1. Pour **salsa** onto **dough.** Use table knife to spread evenly over dough.

2. Crush **nacho chips** with your hands. Sprinkle evenly over pizza.

3. Sprinkle **cheddar** and **mozzarella** or **Monterey jack** evenly over pizza.

4. Arrange **chopped pepper pieces** evenly on pizza.

5. Sprinkle **corn** evenly over pizza.

6. Bake for **20 minutes.** Use pot holders to remove from oven. *Turn off oven.*

7. Wear a sombrero while you eat your Nacho Crush Pie.

PIZZABIT

Back in the pioneer days, young Native Americans were *very* good at keeping their corn crops safe from pests. These smart kids made whistles and hung them on poles in the cornfields. When the wind blew through the whistles, the noise scared birds, mice, and other unwelcome pests from the fields. Those must have been some very musical cornfields!

MAKES ONE 12-INCH PIE

PREHEAT OVEN TO 400°F

INGREDIENTS
1 RECIPE PREPARED PIZZA DOUGH PLACED ON GREASED PIZZA PAN
½ CUP SALSA
ABOUT 15 LARGE NACHO CHIPS
½ CUP GRATED CHEDDAR CHEESE (SEE PAGE 38 FOR ILLUSTRATED TECHNIQUE)
½ CUP GRATED MOZZARELLA OR MONTEREY JACK
½ CUP FROZEN CHOPPED PEPPERS (RED AND GREEN), THAWED
½ CUP FROZEN OR CANNED CORN, THAWED

TOOLS
GREASED PIZZA PAN
MEASURING CUPS
GRATER
TABLE KNIFE
POT HOLDERS

MAKES ONE
12-INCH PIE

PREHEAT OVEN
TO 400°F

INGREDIENTS

1 RECIPE PREPARED
   PIZZA DOUGH
   PLACED ON
   GREASED PIZZA
   PAN
⅓ CUP RICOTTA
   CHEESE
1 LARGE CLOVE GARLIC
4 SLICES PROVOLONE
   CHEESE
2 TABLESPOONS
   GRATED PARME-
   SAN CHEESE

TOOLS

GREASED PIZZA PAN
POT HOLDERS
MEASURING CUPS
   AND SPOONS
TABLE KNIFE
SMALL JUICE GLASS
ROLLING PIN
CLEAN, STURDY
   PLASTIC BAG
CUTTING BOARD

FULL MOON PIE

This is one full moon that's sure to drive your friends wild!

 Bake **dough** in oven for **10 minutes.** Use pot holders to remove from oven. Place on stove. Leave oven on.

 Use table knife to spread **ricotta** evenly over crust.

 Gently crush **garlic clove** with the bottom of the juice glass. Peel garlic clove.

 Do the Garlic Smash. Put garlic clove into clean plastic bag. Pound gently with end of rolling pin. Pound garlic until it is well smashed. (*See page 34 for illustrated technique.*) Sprinkle evenly over pizza.

 Break up **provolone** and arrange evenly on pizza.

 Sprinkle **parmesan** evenly over pizza.

 Bake for **8–10 minutes.** Remove with pot holders. *Turn off oven.*

 Eat a slice of the moon!

CRAZY CRUSTS

Crazy Crusts come in lots of different shapes and sizes. Some are big, some are small, some are twisted, and some are all rolled up. You can fill them, you can stuff them, you can top them with your favorite things. Any way you do it, they're delicious and loads of fun to make.

Experiment with different fillings and toppings on your favorite Crazy Crust shape. Or, experiment with the dough and make your own custom Crazy Crust! (*See page 79 for more topping ideas.*)

MAKES 1
MOON PIE

PREHEAT OVEN
TO 400°F

INGREDIENTS
½ RECIPE-PREPARED
  PIZZA DOUGH
  PLUS SCRAPS
1 TEASPOON OIL
¼ CUP PIZZA SAUCE
⅓ CUP RICOTTA
  CHEESE
½ CUP GRATED MOZ-
  ZARELLA (SEE
  PAGE 38 FOR
  ILLUSTRATED
  TECHNIQUE)
1 TABLESPOON GRAT-
  ED PARMESAN

TOOLS
CLEAN, FLOURED
  SURFACE
ROLLING PIN
CLEAN RULER
GREASED PIZZA PAN
  OR COOKIE SHEET
MEASURING CUPS
  AND SPOONS
TABLE KNIFE
FORK
POT HOLDERS

LOONY MOON PIE
This moon pie is so good you'll howl for more!

1. Roll **dough** into a ball. Put it onto a clean floured surface. Use rolling pin to roll ball into an 8-inch circle. Keep scraps to use later. Put circle onto pizza pan or cookie sheet. *(See page 27 for illustrated technique.)*

2. Pour **oil** onto **dough circle.** Use your fingers to spread oil over dough.

3. Use table knife to spread **sauce** on one half of circle.

4. Spread **ricotta cheese** on top of sauce.

PIZZABIT

Moon Pie is another name for a calzone — a half-moon shaped turnover stuffed with cheese, vegetables, and meat, or a combination of any two or all three. But calzones didn't always look like half moons. In fact, they started out as long stuffed tubes of dough, and looked like the baggy pants that men wore in the Eighteenth Century. In Italian calzone means "pant legs." Guess we could call this recipe "Pant Leg Pie"! Nah...

5. Sprinkle **mozzarella** and **parmesan** onto ricotta.

6. Gently lift plain edge of the circle. Fold the circle in half. Pinch the edges shut. Next, use a fork to press edges together.

7. Use **dough scraps** to make a loony face on your moon pie.

8. Poke moon pie 3 or 4 times with fork.

9. Bake for **20 minutes.** Use pot holders to remove from oven. *Turn off oven.*

10. Do something loony while you eat your Loony Moon Pie!

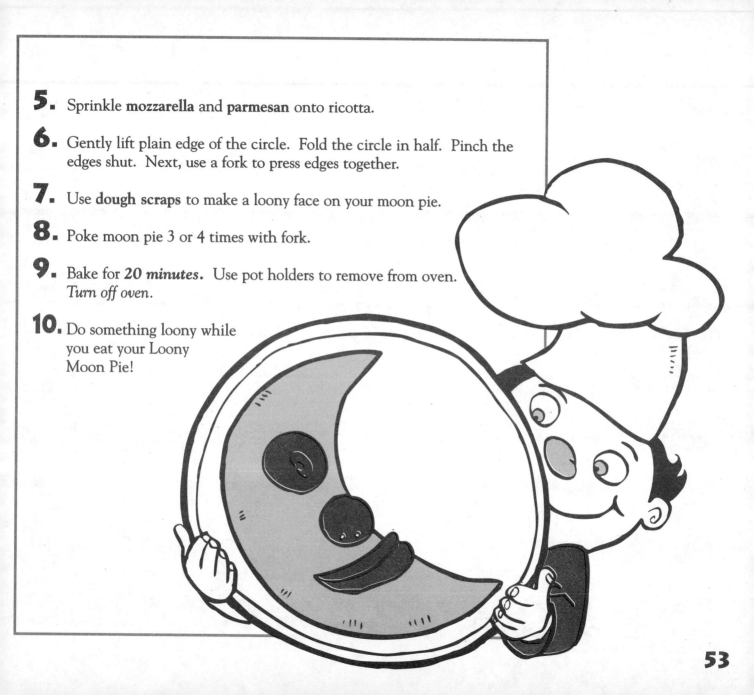

HOW TO STUFF A MOON PIE

1. Use rolling pin to roll dough into 8-inch circle. (Or into 4-inch circles if making Mini-Moon pies.)

2. Put circle(s) on cookie sheet.

3. Spread sauce onto one half of circle. Leave at least a ¼-inch sauce-free edge.

4. Cover the same half of the circle with cheeses and other fillings. Leave the other half plain.

5. Lift plain edge of circle and fold over to other edge.

6. Use your fingers to pinch edges shut.

7. Use a fork to press edges shut. Be sure edges are shut tightly.

8. Use dough scraps to make a loony face on the moon pie.

9. Poke with fork in three or four different places.

10. Bake as directed.

MANY MINI-MOON PIES

Here's one way to make many Mini-Moon Pies
— it's up to you to think up many, many more.

 1 Put **ricotta cheese** and **swiss cheese** into the mixing bowl. Use fork to mix well.

 2 Break **ham** into little pieces. Put in bowl. Use fork to mix well.

 3 Put the **dough** onto the clean floured surface. Divide into ten golf ball-sized balls.

 4 Roll each **dough ball** into a small circle, about 4 inches wide. Put circles onto cookie sheet.

 5 Put **1 tablespoon of cheese-ham mixture** onto one half of each circle.

 6 Gently lift plain edge of each circle and fold over to other side. Use your fingers and fork to shut tightly. Repeat with each circle.

 7 Poke each Mini-Moon pie three times with fork.

 8 Bake for **15 minutes.** Use pot holders to remove from oven. *Turn off oven.*

 MAKES 10 MINI-MOON PIES

 PREHEAT OVEN TO 400°F

INGREDIENTS
½ CUP RICOTTA CHEESE
¼ CUP SHREDDED SWISS CHEESE (SEE PAGE 38 FOR ILLUSTRATED TECHNIQUE)
2 PIECES DELI-SLICED HAM
1 RECIPE DOUGH

TOOLS
MEASURING CUPS AND SPOONS
SMALL MIXING BOWL
FORK
CLEAN, FLOURED SURFACE
ROLLING PIN
CLEAN RULER
GREASED COOKIE SHEET
POT HOLDERS

9 Eat as many Mini-Moon Pies as you like.

DREAM UP YOUR OWN
MINI-MOON PIE COMBINATIONS...

PEPPERONI AND PEPPERS

CHILIES AND CHEDDAR

MUSHROOMS AND MOZZARELLA

TOMATOES AND CHEESE

VEGGIE WEDGIES
Incredibly Edible Wedgetables!

 MAKES 4 WEDGIES

PREHEAT OVEN
TO 400°F

1. Put **dough** onto clean, floured surface. Use rolling pin to roll into an 8-inch circle.

2. Cut **dough circle** in half. Next, cut both halves in half to form four triangles. Put triangles on cookie sheet.

3. Put **carrots, broccoli, cottage cheese,** and **cheddar cheese** into the mixing bowl. Mix well.

4. Spread **1 teaspoon sauce** on each triangle.

5. Put about **½ cup of vegetable-cheese mixture** on each triangle. Spread evenly over triangle.

6. Bake for **15–20 minutes.** Use pot holders to remove from oven. *Turn off oven.*

7. Veggies never tasted this good!

INGREDIENTS
½ RECIPE OF PREPARED
   PIZZA DOUGH
½ CUP GRATED CARROT
   — ABOUT 2 CARROTS
   (SEE PAGE 38 FOR
   ILLUSTRATED
   TECHNIQUE)
½ CUP FROZEN CHOPPED
   BROCCOLI, THAWED
½ CUP COTTAGE CHEESE
¼ CUP GRATED
   CHEDDAR CHEESE
4 TEASPOONS PIZZA
   SAUCE

TOOLS
CLEAN, FLOURED
   SURFACE
ROLLING PIN
TABLE KNIFE
GRATER
CLEAN RULER
GREASED COOKIE SHEET
MEASURING CUPS AND
   SPOONS
MIXING BOWL
WOODEN SPOON
POT HOLDERS

MAKES 1
STROMBOLI

PREHEAT OVEN
TO 400°F

INGREDIENTS
½ RECIPE OF PRE-
PARED PIZZA
DOUGH
1 TEASPOON OIL
2 TABLESPOONS PIZZA
SAUCE
4 PIECES DELI-SLICED
HAM
½ CUP GRATED MOZ-
ZARELLA (SEE
PAGE 38 FOR
ILLUSTRATED
TECHNIQUE)

TOOLS
CLEAN, FLOURED
SURFACE
ROLLING PIN
CLEAN RULER
GREASED COOKIE
SHEET
MEASURING CUPS
AND SPOONS
TABLE KNIFE
FORK
POT HOLDERS

ROLLY STROMBOLI
Holy moley! It's a Rolly Stromboli!

 Put **dough** on clean, floured surface. Use rolling pin to roll dough into long rectangle — 12–15 inches long, 8 inches wide.

 Fold dough in half. Put on cookie sheet. Unfold dough.

 Pour **oil** onto dough. Use your fingers to spread oil over entire piece of dough.

 Pour **sauce** onto dough. Use table knife to spread over entire piece of dough.

 Arrange **ham** evenly over dough.

 Sprinkle **mozzarella** evenly over dough.

 Carefully roll up rectangle, from long edge to long edge. You should make a long thick stick (*see page 60 for illustrated technique*).

 Pinch edges shut.

9 Poke with fork in five to six different places.

10 Bake for **20 minutes.** Use pot holders to remove from oven. *Turn off oven.*

11 Munch!

HOW TO ROLL A ROLLY STROMBOLI

1. Put dough on clean floured surface. Use your hands and fingers to flatten and stretch dough into a square.

2. Use rolling pin to roll out dough into a long rectangle. First roll out dough to make it as long as you can. Sprinkle with flour to keep dough from sticking.

3. Next, roll out dough the other way to make it wider. Keep rolling out dough until it is 12–15 inches long and about 8 inches wide. Don't worry if you can't make a perfect rectangle.

4. Fold dough in half. Put on cookie sheet. Unfold the dough.

5. Spread and arrange fillings evenly on dough.

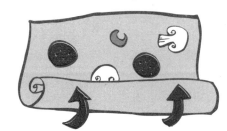

6. Grab one of the long edges (12–15 inches) with your fingers. Roll this edge towards the other long edge to make a long thick stick.

7. Pinch edges shut.

8. Poke with fork in five to six different places.

9. Bake as directed.

MAKES 12 MUFFIN
STUFFER CUPS

PREHEAT OVEN
TO 400°F

INGREDIENTS
1 RECIPE PREPARED
    NIFTY JIFFY DOUGH
12 TEASPOONS PIZZA
    SAUCE
6 TEASPOONS RICOTTA
    CHEESE
½ CUP FROZEN
    CHOPPED SPINACH
    OR OTHER GREEN
    VEGETABLE, THAWED
½ CUP FROZEN OR
    CANNED CORN,
    THAWED
12 TABLESPOONS GRAT-
    ED MOZZARELLA
    (SEE PAGE 38
    FOR ILLUSTRATED
    TECHNIQUE)

TOOLS
GREASED MUFFIN PAN
MEASURING CUPS AND
    SPOONS
SMALL BOWL
MIXING SPOON
GRATER
POT HOLDERS

PIZZA MUFFIN STUFFER CUPS
Nothin' like a Pizza Muffin Stuffer Cup!

 Divide **dough** into 12 equal pieces and roll each piece into a ball about the size of a ping pong ball.

 Put each **dough ball** into a separate cup of the muffin pan. Next, press each ball with your fingers to spread the dough on the bottom and sides of the muffin cups. You should have twelve dough cups when you're done.

 Put **1 teaspoon sauce** into each **dough cup**. Spread onto bottom and sides.

 Put **½ teaspoon ricotta** into each dough cup. Use your fingers to scrape the ricotta off the measuring spoon.

 Put **spinach** and **corn** into the small bowl. Mix well.

 Put **1 tablespoon of the spinach-corn mixture** into each dough cup.

 Put approximately **1 tablespoon of mozzarella** into each muffin cup.

8 Bake for **15–20 minutes** or until crust is golden and cheese is bubbly. Use pot holders to remove from oven. *Turn off oven.*

9 Stuff a Muffin Stuffer Cup in your mouth.

MAKES 1
DIMPLE DISC

PREHEAT OVEN
TO 400°F

INGREDIENTS
1 RECIPE PREPARED
    PIZZA DOUGH
¼ CUP GRATED
    PARMESAN CHEESE
1 TEASPOON DRIED
    OREGANO
1 TEASPOON DRIED
    ROSEMARY
1 TEASPOON DRIED
    BASIL
2 TEASPOONS OLIVE
    OIL
3 TABLESPOONS PIZZA
    SAUCE

TOOLS
LARGE MIXING BOWL
MEASURING CUPS
    AND SPOONS
GREASED COOKIE
    SHEET OR PIZZA
    PAN
CLEAN RULER
TABLE KNIFE
POT HOLDERS

THICK AND CHEWY DIMPLE DISC
This pie has such cute dimples!

1 Put **dough** into the mixing bowl. Add **parmesan, oregano, rosemary,** and **basil.** Use your hands to mix and knead the cheese and spices into the dough.

2 Roll **spiced dough** into a ball and put onto a greased cookie sheet or pizza pan. Next, flatten dough into a circle about 6–8 inches wide.

3 Now dimple the dough (this is the fun part!). Poke dough to make small dents (or dimples) all over top of dough. Be careful not to poke all the way through the dough.

4 Pour **oil** onto dough and use your fingers to spread it evenly over dough.

PIZZABIT

Dimple Disc is really just another word for focaccia (pronounced fō-cot-cha). Focaccia is a thick round piece of baked dough. Some creative Italian cooks love to make focaccia more interesting by **adding cheeses, olives, spices, and vegetables to the dough.**

Pour **sauce** onto dough. Use table knife to spread sauce evenly over dough.

 Bake for **20–25 minutes** until golden brown. Use pot holders to remove from oven. *Turn off oven.*

 Get creative with your next Dimple Disc and make it doubly delicious!

TWISTED PIZZA CHEWS

Tasty chews for choosy chewers!

🔪 MAKES APPROXI-
MATELY 20 CHEWS

🍪 PREHEAT OVEN
TO 400°F

INGREDIENTS

1 RECIPE PREPARED
   DIVINE OR
   DYNAMO DOUGH
½ CUP PIZZA SAUCE
1¼ CUPS GRATED
   PARMESAN CHEESE

TOOLS

CLEAN, FLOURED
   SURFACE
CLEAN RULER
TABLE KNIFE
MEASURING CUPS
SPOON
2 CEREAL BOWLS
GREASED COOKIE
   SHEET, SPRINKLED
   WITH CORNMEAL
POT HOLDERS

1. Divide **dough** into four equal balls.

2. Roll each **dough ball** into a long skinny "snake," about 20 inches long. Next, cut each "snake" into four or five "worms," about 5 inches long.

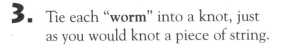

3. Tie each "**worm**" into a knot, just as you would knot a piece of string.

4. Put **pizza sauce** into one cereal bowl and the **parmesan cheese** into the other.

5. Roll each **dough knot** in as much pizza sauce as possible. Next, roll in the cheese. Put on cookie sheet. Repeat with all knots.

6. Bake for *10–12 minutes.* Check often to make sure pizza chews don't burn. Use pot holders to remove from oven. *Turn off oven.*

7. Figure out how many chews it takes to chew a Twisted Pizza Chew!

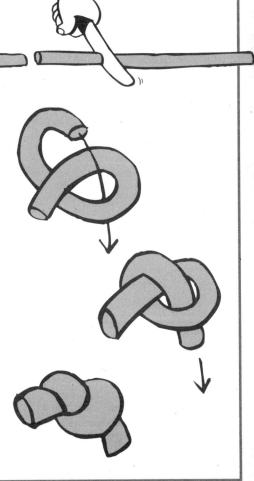

SWEETIE PIES

Sweetie Pies are great for desserts, snacks, and some you can even eat for breakfast! The recipes in this section are all for 12-inch pies, made from either Sweetie Pie Dough (page 24) or Nifty Jiffy Dough (page 26). Sweetie Pie toppings are also great on ready-made pie crusts. So, sharpen your sweet tooth and start baking! (*See page 79 for more topping ideas.*)

PURPLEBERRY SMASH AND SQUISH PIE

A blueberry pie gone purple!

MAKES ONE
12-INCH PIE

PREHEAT OVEN
TO 400°F

INGREDIENTS

1 RECIPE PREPARED
    SWEETIE PIE OR
    NIFTY JIFFY
    DOUGH PLACED
    ON GREASED
    PIZZA PAN
½ CUP CREAM CHEESE
¼ CUP ALL-FRUIT
    BLUEBERRY JAM
1 CUP FRESH OR
    FROZEN BLUEBER-
    RIES, THAWED
1 TABLESPOON FLOUR
1 TABLESPOON SUGAR

TOOLS

GREASED PIZZA PAN
POT HOLDERS
MEASURING CUPS
    AND SPOONS
SMALL BOWL
FORK
RUBBER SPATULA OR
    LARGE SPOON
TABLE KNIFE
CLEAN, PLASTIC BAG
    (A BREAD BAG IS
    PERFECT)

 Bake **dough** for **5 minutes.** Use pot holders to remove from oven. Leave oven on.

 Put **cream cheese** and **jam** into small bowl. Use fork to mix well.

 Use spatula or spoon to scoop **cream cheese-jam mixture** onto crust. Spread evenly over crust.

 Put **blueberries, flour,** and **sugar** into small bowl.

Do the Purpleberry Smash and Squish. Put clean plastic bag over your hand like a glove. Using your bagged hand, smash, squish, and squeeze the berries. Squish them until they're good and gooey.

 Use a spoon to spread **smashed blueberries** evenly over pizza.

 Bake for **15 minutes.** Use pot holders to remove from oven. *Turn off oven.*

 Have a Purpleberry Smash and Squish Bash!

NANA CREAM PIE

Go bananas!

- MAKES ONE 12-INCH PIE
- PREHEAT OVEN TO 400°F

1. Bake **dough** for *5 minutes*. Use pot holders to remove from oven. Leave oven on.

2. Put **ricotta** and **sugar** into small mixing bowl. Mix well.

3. Spoon **ricotta mixture** onto crust. Use table knife to spread evenly over crust.

4. Cut **bananas** into very skinny slices. Put into small mixing bowl. Add **maple syrup.** Stir gently with small spoon.

INGREDIENTS
1 RECIPE PREPARED
    SWEETIE PIE OR
    NIFTY JIFFY
    DOUGH PLACED
    ON GREASED
    PIZZA PAN
½ CUP RICOTTA
    CHEESE
2 TABLESPOONS
    SUGAR
2–3 LARGE BANANAS
2 TABLESPOONS
    MAPLE SYRUP

TOOLS
GREASED PIZZA PAN
POT HOLDERS
MEASURING CUPS
    AND SPOONS
2 SMALL MIXING
    BOWLS
LARGE SPOON
TABLE KNIFE
SMALL SPOON

PIZZABIT

Did you know that banana plants are one of the largest non-wood plants on earth? Banana plants can grow as high as 25 feet. (That's taller than three very tall basketball players standing on top of each other!)

A banana plant produces one stem of bananas, or about 140 bananas. That's a lot of monkey food! When the bananas are ready to be sent to market, the whole banana plant is cut down so that another one can grow in its place.

5. Use your fingers to arrange **banana slices** evenly over pizza. Try to cover entire pizza with banana slices.

6. Bake in oven for *15 minutes*. Use pot holders to remove from oven. *Turn off oven.*

7. Act like a monkey as you eat this treat!

MAKES ONE
12-INCH PIE

PREHEAT OVEN
TO 400°F

INGREDIENTS

1 RECIPE PREPARED
NIFTY JIFFY
DOUGH
⅓ CUP CHOCOLATE
CHIPS
1 CUP RICOTTA
CHEESE
3 TABLESPOONS
CHOCOLATE
DRINK POWDER

TOOLS

LARGE MIXING BOWL
MEASURING CUPS
AND SPOONS
CLEAN, FLOURED
SURFACE
ROLLING PIN
GREASED 12-INCH
PIZZA PAN OR
COOKIE SHEET
POT HOLDERS
SPOON
SMALL BOWL
RUBBER SPATULA OR
LARGE SPOON

CHOCO-LATTA CHIP PIE

A chocolate-lover's pizza pie.

 Put **dough** and **chocolate chips** into mixing bowl. Use your hands to mix chips into dough. Mix well. Form dough into a ball.

 Put **chocolate chip dough** onto clean, floured surface. Knead for *1 minute.* (*See page 20 for illustrated technique.*)

 Roll dough to fit pizza pan or cookie sheet. (*See page 27 for illustrated technique.*) Carefully lift and place onto pan.

 Bake for **5 minutes.** Use pot holders to remove from oven. Leave oven on.

 Put **ricotta** and **chocolate drink mix** into the small bowl. Mix well.

 Use rubber spatula or large spoon to spread **ricotta-chocolate mixture** evenly over crust.

 Bake for **10 minutes.** Use pot holders to remove from oven. *Turn off oven.*

Serve this with ice cream and you'll have Chilly Choco-Latta Chip Pie!

73

MAKES ONE
12-INCH PIE

PREHEAT OVEN
TO 400°F

INGREDIENTS
1 RECIPE PREPARED
    NIFTY JIFFY OR
    SWEETIE PIE
    DOUGH ON
    GREASED PIZZA
    PAN
6 SMALL PEACHES
1 TABLESPOON SUGAR
2 TABLESPOONS
    FLOUR
¼ TEASPOON CINNA-
    MON
½ CUP FLOUR
½ CUP ROLLED OATS
    (NOT INSTANT)
¼ CUP SOFTENED
    BUTTER OR
    MARGARINE
¼ CUP BROWN SUGAR
1 TABLESPOON WATER

TOOLS
GREASED PIZZA PAN
CUTTING BOARD
SHARP KNIFE
MIXING BOWL
MEASURING CUPS
    AND SPOONS
SPOON
POT HOLDERS
ADULT HELPER

PEACHY KEEN PIE

The peachiest pizza you've ever tasted!

1. Bake **dough** for **5 minutes.** Use pot holders to remove from oven. Leave oven on.

2. Put **peaches** on the cutting board. Ask an adult to cut peaches into very skinny slices.

3. Put **peach slices, sugar, 2 tablespoons flour,** and **cinnamon** into mixing bowl. Mix gently.

4. Spread **peach mixture** evenly over pizza crust.

5. Put **½ cup flour, oats, butter or margarine, brown sugar,** and **water** into mixing bowl. Use your clean hands to squish the ingredients together until they are well mixed.

6. Pinch off little bits of **oat-butter mixture** and sprinkle onto pizza. Do this until you've used up all of the oat-butter mixture. Cover pizza evenly with mixture.

7. Bake for **15 minutes.** Use pot holders to remove from oven. *Turn off oven.*

8. Enjoy!

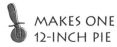

MAKES ONE
12-INCH PIE

PREHEAT OVEN
TO 400°F

INGREDIENTS
1 RECIPE PREPARED
   NIFTY JIFFY OR
   SWEETIE PIE
   DOUGH ON
   GREASED PIZZA
   PAN
⅓ CUP ALL-FRUIT
   STRAWBERRY JAM
1½ CUPS STRAW-
   BERRIES
1 TABLESPOON SUGAR

TOOLS
GREASED PIZZA PAN
POT HOLDERS
MEASURING CUPS
   AND SPOONS
CEREAL BOWL
SPOON
TABLE KNIFE
CUTTING BOARD
ADULT HELPER

STICKY STRAWBERRY PIE
Sticky-licking good!

 Bake **dough** for **10 minutes.** Use pot holders to remove from oven. *Turn off oven.*

 Put **strawberry jam** into cereal bowl. Stir well to soften.

 Use table knife to spread jam evenly over pizza crust.

 Pick green stems off **strawberries.** Next, put strawberries on cutting board. Cut into very skinny pieces. (You may want to ask an adult to help you with a sharp knife.)

PIZZABIT

How many pieces of fruit do you eat when you eat one red strawberry? Dozens! One strawberry is actually many fruits in one. Just take a good look at a strawberry. See all of the tiny specks covering the strawberry? Each of those specks is actually a tiny fruit, called an achene.

Arrange **sliced strawberries** evenly on pizza.

 Sprinkle **sugar** onto strawberries.

 Bake for **8–10 minutes.** Ask adult to help you remove from oven. Set on stove to cool completely (about **30 minutes**). *Turn off oven.*

 You'll need a napkin for this one!

MAKES ONE
12-INCH PIE

PREHEAT OVEN
TO 400°F

INGREDIENTS
1 RECIPE PREPARED
    SWEETIE PIE OR
    NIFTY JIFFY
    DOUGH PLACED
    ON GREASED PAN
1 CUP APPLESAUCE
½ CUP CREAM CHEESE
1 TABLESPOON SUGAR
2 TABLESPOONS
    RAISINS
¼ TEASPOON
    CINNAMON

TOOLS
GREASED PIZZA PAN
POT HOLDERS
MEASURING CUPS
    AND SPOONS
SMALL MIXING BOWL
FORK
RUBBER SPATULA OR
    LARGE SPOON

APPLESAUCE PIE
Perfect for Saturday morning breakfast or a late Friday night snack!

1. Bake **dough** for **5 minutes.** Use pot holders to remove from oven. Leave oven on.

2. Put **applesauce** and **cream cheese** into the mixing bowl. Use fork to mix well.

3. Add **sugar, raisins,** and **cinnamon** to **applesauce-cream cheese mixture.** Mix well.

4. Use spatula or spoon to scoop mixture onto crust. Spread evenly over crust.

5. Bake for **15 minutes.** Use pot holders to remove from oven. *Turn off oven.*

6. Mmmm. This one tastes like it came from the bakery!

PIZZABIT

There are more than 7,500 different kinds of apples grown in the world and 2,500 of those varieties are grown in America!

The eight most popular apples in America are: Macintosh, Red Delicious, Golden Delicious, Granny Smith, Jonathan, Rome Beauty, Stayman, and York. Which kind is your favorite?

TOPS & BOTTOMS FOR EVERY KIND OF PIZZA PIE

Making pizza is fun — especially when you design a pie all by yourself. Here's a list of cheeses, sauces, vegetables, fruits, sweets, and crusts which you can use to create your own pizza masterpiece or a personalized pie for a special friend or family member.

BOTTOMS

Bagels ◆ Crackers ◆ Croissants ◆ English muffins ◆ Hamburger buns
Hard rolls ◆ Homemade pizza doughs ◆ Italian or French bread ◆ Pita breads
Store-bought pie crusts ◆ Store-bought pizza crusts ◆ Store-bought biscuit dough
Soft tortillas ◆ Taco shells ◆ Tostadas

SAUCES

Crushed tomato ◆ Cheese sauce
Oil and Garlic ◆ Pesto ◆ Pizza sauce
Salsa ◆ Spaghetti sauce

CHEESES

American ◆ Blue ◆ Cheddar ◆ Cottage
Cream ◆ Feta ◆ Monterey Jack
Mozzarella ◆ Parmesan ◆ Provolone
Ricotta ◆ Soy ◆ Swiss

MEATS AND FISH

Anchovies ◆ Bacon (pre-cooked) ◆ Chicken (pre-cooked) ◆ Canadian bacon
Ground beef (pre-cooked) ◆ Ground turkey (pre-cooked) ◆ Ham
Meatball (pre-cooked) ◆ Pepperoni ◆ Roast beef ◆ Salami ◆ Sardines
Sausage (pre-cooked) ◆ Scallops ◆ Shrimp ◆ Tuna fish

Note: Make sure *all* raw meat and fish is either pre-cooked or cooked thoroughly through during the pizza baking time.

VEGETABLES

Asparagus ◆ Beans ◆ Broccoli ◆ Carrots ◆ Cauliflower ◆ Collard greens
Corn ◆ Mushrooms (sautéed in oil) ◆ Olives ◆ Onions (raw or sautéed in oil)
Peas ◆ Peppers ◆ Potatoes ◆ Spinach
Squash ◆ Tomatoes ◆ Zucchini

HERBS AND SPICES

Basil ◆ Chili peppers ◆ Chili powder ◆ Garlic ◆ Oregano ◆ Parsley

SWEETS AND NUTS

All-fruit jams ◆ Almonds ◆ Apples
Applesauce ◆ Apple butter
Bananas ◆ Berries ◆ Cashews
Cherries ◆ Chocolate ◆ Dates
Figs ◆ Grapes ◆ Honey ◆ Ice cream
Kiwi fruit ◆ Maple syrup
Peaches ◆ Peanuts ◆ Peanut butter
Pears ◆ Pecans ◆ Plums ◆ Prunes
Pudding ◆ Raisins ◆ Sesame seeds
Walnuts

OTHER GOOD STUFF

Cereals ◆ Nacho chips ◆ Potato chips
Spaghetti ◆ Your favorite food

INDEX